THE UNOFFICIAL
A COURT OF THORNS AND ROSES
COCKTAIL BOOK

THE UNOFFICIAL
A COURT OF THORNS AND ROSES
COCKTAIL BOOK

J. BECKER

Andrews McMeel
PUBLISHING®

CONTENTS

INTRODUCTION
1

TOOLS FOR YOUR JOURNEY
3

GLASSWARE
5

COCKTAIL & MOCKTAIL INGREDIENTS
6

INFUSED SPIRITS
11

RECIPE INDEX
17

COCKTAILS AND MOCKTAILS
19

PREFERRED BUBBLY OF THE COURTS
105

SNACKS AND SPREADS
107

PAIRINGS TO ENTERTAIN
121

Welcome to the enchanting world of Prythian, with cocktails and snacks inspired by *A Court of Thorns and Roses*. The fantastical, magical universe of Sarah J. Maas is intoxicating on its own, but if you wish to truly immerse yourself in the world of the fae, this book is your guide through the drinks, drafts, and lore of Prythian.

In these pages, you'll find a collection of creative yet approachable cocktails that capture the essence of the series' beloved characters, otherworldly settings, and breathtaking moments. Whether you're toasting to the Cursebreaker, celebrating a solstice, or unwinding with your found family, there's a cocktail or mocktail here for every fan.

In each recipe, we pay homage to the incredible world that Maas has built in *A Court of Thorns and Roses, A Court of Mist and Fury, A Court of Wings and Ruin, A Court of Frost and Starlight*, and *A Court of Silver Flames*.

Journey through the sips and bites of Prythian

In these enchanting pages, you'll discover 46 cocktail and mocktail recipes and six additional infused spirits. You'll be able to relive the beloved scenes and treasured moments in the faerie world once again. Following the sips, you'll find six plates to enjoy alongside the libations.

On page 121, you'll find suggested drink and food pairings for your next gathering of like-minded book lovers. However, rules are made to be broken, so enjoy the contents of this book however you please!

Tools for Your Journey

Shaker
The most common at-home style is the cobbler shaker. This shaker consists of a tumbler base, a lid with a strainer, and a cap to go over the lid for mess-free concoction shaking.

Cocktail Strainer
Though the cobbler-style shaker has a built-in strainer, there are certain cocktails (anything muddled with fruits or herbs in the shaker) that need an extra strain. These have a handle and generally fit snugly in the tumbler base of a cocktail shaker.

Liquid Measuring Glass
A measuring glass with ½ fluid ounce gradations or a stainless steel jigger with ½ fluid ounce gradations will do. I prefer the former.

Channel Knife or Vegetable Peeler
Used to cut a citrus fruit peel into a twist. *(And who doesn't love a good twist?)*

Cocktail Muddler
Used to muddle fruit in the bottom of a shaker or cocktail glass.

Bar Spoon
Used to stir to combine cocktails in the glass they are served.

GLASSWARE

It's common that the volume can vary for the glasses you have in your cabinet or on your bar cart, so you may find yourself adding a few more cubes of ice to a glass or with a little extra liquid in your shaker.

MARTINI GLASS—Holds 6 to 8 fluid ounces
COUPE GLASS—Holds 5 to 8 fluid ounces
CHAMPAGNE FLUTE—Holds 6 to 7 fluid ounces
WINE GLASS—Holds 12 to 16 fluid ounces
MARTINI GLASS—Holds 6 to 8 fluid ounces
ROCKS GLASS—Holds 7 to 12 fluid ounces
HIGHBALL GLASS—Holds 8 to 12 fluid ounces
COLLINS GLASS—Holds 10 to 14 fluid ounces
PINT GLASS—Holds 16 fluid ounces
MUG—Holds 8 to 12 fluid ounces

Cocktail & Mocktail Ingredients

If you'd like to crack the spine of this book and make every cocktail and mocktail listed, you'll need to stock your bar, pantry, and refrigerator with the following ingredients:

ALCOHOL

Amaretto

Bourbon

Bourbon cherries (such as Woodford Reserve Bourbon Cherries)

Coffee liqueur (such as Kahlúa)

Crème de violette

Dark rum

Dry vermouth

Elderflower liqueur (such as St-Germain)

Gin

Guinness

Irish cream (such as Baileys Irish Cream or a homemade version)

Irish pilsner (such as Harp)

Italian bitter liqueur (such as Aperol)

Limoncello

Maraschino liqueur

Orange bitters

Orange liqueur (such as Cointreau or Grand Marnier)

Peppermint schnapps

Pimm's No. 1 liqueur

Prosecco

Silver tequila

Vodka

Whiskey

NONALCOHOLIC MIXERS AND GARNISHES

Amaretto syrup

Apple juice (such as Martinelli's or Simply Apple)

Black pepper

Celery seed

Chai tea bags

Chocolate syrup

Cinnamon (ground and stick)

Club soda

Cocoa powder

Coffee

Cranberry juice

Dark chocolate

Earl Grey tea bags

Edible glitter

Elderflower syrup

Espresso beans

Ginger ale

Ginger beer

Grenadine

Gummy worm

Heavy cream

Hibiscus syrup (such as Monin Hibiscus Syrup)

Hot honey (such as Mike's Hot Honey)

Hot sauce

Instant coffee

Jasmine green tea bags

Lavender syrup (such as Monin Lavender Syrup)

Lemon-lime soda

Lemonade

Maple syrup

Milk

Mint tea bags (such as Numi Moroccan Mint tea)

Olives in brine

Peppermint syrup

Pickled pepperoncini

Pineapple juice

Pomegranate juice

Rose syrup

Rose tea bags

Sea salt

Seasoned salt

Simple syrup

Sparkling apple cider (such as Martinelli's)

Strawberry jam

Sugar

Sweetened condensed milk

Tart cherry juice

Tomato juice

Vanilla extract

Vanilla syrup (such as Monin Vanilla Syrup)

Worcestershire sauce

Produce

Apple

Basil

Blackberries

Cherry

Cucumber

Grapefruit

Jalapeño

Lemon

Lime

Mint

Orange

Pomegranate seeds

Rosemary

Strawberry

Infused Spirits

Jasmine Green Tea–Infused Gin

INGREDIENTS

   6 fluid ounces gin

   2 jasmine green tea bags

METHOD

Steep in room-temperature gin for 1 hour.

Rose Tea–Infused Vodka

INGREDIENTS

   6 fluid ounces vodka

   2 rose tea bags

METHOD

Steep in room-temperature vodka for 1 hour.

Rose Tea–Infused Gin

INGREDIENTS

   6 fluid ounces gin

   2 rose tea bags

METHOD

Steep in room-temperature vodka for 1 hour.

CHAI TEA–INFUSED BOURBON

INGREDIENTS

    6 fluid ounces bourbon

    2 chai tea bags

METHOD

Steep in room-temperature bourbon for 1 hour.

BLACKBERRY-INFUSED WHISKEY

INGREDIENTS

    6 fluid ounces whiskey

    8 to 10 blackberries

METHOD

Combine and place in a sealed container. Refrigerate for 4 to 8 hours.

Recipe for Homemade Irish Cream

    1 (14-fluid ounce) can of sweetened condensed milk

    1½ cups Irish whiskey

    1 cup heavy cream

    2 tablespoons chocolate syrup

    1 teaspoon instant coffee

    1 teaspoon vanilla extract

METHOD

Add all ingredients to a blender and blend until combined. Store in an airtight container.

UNOFFICIAL
A COURT OF THORNS AND ROSES
RECIPE INDEX

Feyre Darling. 21

Tamlin Tequila Cocktail 23

The Vulgar Gesture 25

Lucien's Cocktail 27

Elain's Garden 29

Elain's Garden Mocktail 31

Pool of Starlight 33

Faerie Wine in the Spring Court . . 35

The Rhysand 37

Amarantha. 39

Under the Mountain Mocktail 41

Nesta's Dirty Martini. 43

The Wyrm 45

Winter Solstice in the
    Spring Court 47

The Night Court 49

Rhysand's Calming Tea 51

Sweet Scent of Freedom 53

Mor's Citrus and Cinnamon 55

Summer Court Wine 57

The Cassian 59

The Azriel 61

The Bloody Amren 63

Mint Tea Julep. 65

Chilled Mint Tea Mocktail 67

Summer Court Mocktail. 69

The Invisible Speck of Lint 71

Starfall Celebration Cocktail. 73

The Blood Ruby. 75

The Court of Dreams Cocktail 77

Rose Tea Lemonade Cocktail 79

Rose Tea Lemonade Mocktail. 81

The Court of Nightmares 83

Winter Court Cocktail 85

Winter Court Mocktail. 87

Illyrian Black and Tan Ale. 89

Helion's Cocktail 91

Soothing Bourbon Cocktail. 93

The Dawn Court 95

Autumn Court Cocktail 97

Autumn Court Mocktail. 99

Valkyrie Vodka Soda 101

Winter Solstice Hot Cocoa. 103

Preferred Bubbly of the Courts . . . 105

COCKTAILS
AND
MOCKTAILS

FEYRE DARLING

Feyre Archeron is anything but fragile. Mortal or Fae, she is capable of not only surviving but flourishing. There are many layers forged together to create a strong, capable woman. If you give her wings, she'll soar. As if painted by Feyre herself, the violet hue of this cocktail will have you looking into her mate's eyes for eternity.

INGREDIENTS

> 2 fluid ounces gin
> ¼ fluid ounce maraschino liqueur
> ½ fluid ounce crème de violette
> ½ fluid ounce lemon juice, freshly squeezed
> Lemon twist for garnish

METHOD

In a cocktail shaker filled three-quarters with ice, add gin, maraschino liqueur, crème de violette, and lemon juice. Shake vigorously for 30 seconds. Strain into a coupe glass and garnish with a lemon twist.

TAMLIN TEQUILA COCKTAIL

Just like its namesake, this tequila cocktail may start off sweet, but there is fury that builds under the surface. Tamlin towers with honey-golden hair and eyes of green, and this cocktail is perfect to showcase the details that make up the High Lord of the Spring Court.

TIP: *You have to dissolve the honey in the un-chilled tequila before adding ice, or you'll have a globby hot (honey) mess.*

INGREDIENTS

  2 fluid ounces silver tequila (room temperature)
  1 tablespoon hot honey (such as Mike's Hot Honey)
  1 fluid ounce lemon juice, freshly squeezed
  3 large basil leaves, and more for garnish
  1 slice of jalapeño, for garnish

METHOD

In an empty shaker, add tequila, hot honey, and lemon juice. Stir with a bar spoon until the honey is completely dissolved. Fill shaker with ice and add basil leaves. Shake for 30 seconds and strain into a martini glass. Garnish with basil leaves and jalapeño.

THE VULGAR GESTURE

This perfect gesture communicates what a Shakespearean volley of insults never could. Here's the perfect drink with the same je ne sais quoi.

INGREDIENTS

1½ fluid ounces silver tequila
½ fluid ounce Italian bitter liqueur (such as Aperol)
½ fluid ounce maraschino liqueur
¾ fluid ounce lime juice, freshly squeezed
Lime slice, for garnish

METHOD

Fill a shaker three-quarters with ice. Then add the silver tequila, Italian bitter liqueur, maraschino liqueur, and lime juice. Shake vigorously for 30 to 60 seconds, then strain into a coupe glass. Garnish with a slice of lime.

LUCIEN'S COCKTAIL

This cocktail dedicated to Lucien may surprise you. Like the Fae himself, it is full of revelations. Though this combination might seem like an obvious nod to his luscious red hair, you should wonder why a faerie cocktail from the Autumn Court feels a little more like a warm–weather cocktail. Perhaps best enjoyed sitting outside on a warm Day (Court).

INGREDIENTS

2 fluid ounces Italian bitter liqueur (such as Aperol)
5 fluid ounces prosecco
1 fluid ounce club soda
Orange slice, for garnish

METHOD

Fill a wine glass with ice. Add Italian bitter liqueur, followed by prosecco, and top with club soda. Garnish with an orange slice.

ELAIN'S GARDEN

This cocktail, inspired by Elain herself, is sweet (but not saccharine) and filled with all the aromas and tastes of a beautiful courtyard garden. Put on your gardening apron and be whisked away to a bewitching garden fit for Fae.

INGREDIENTS

    2 fluid ounces rose tea–infused gin (recipe on page 11)
    ½ fluid ounce elderflower liqueur (such as St-Germaine)
    ½ fluid ounce crème de violette
    ½ fluid ounce maraschino liqueur
    ½ fluid ounce lemon juice, freshly squeezed
    1 teaspoon strawberry jam
    2 fluid ounces club soda
    Strawberry slice and basil leaves, for garnish

METHOD

Fill a cocktail shaker halfway with ice, then add the infused gin, elderflower liqueur, crème de violette, maraschino liqueur, lemon juice, and strawberry jam. Shake for 15 to 30 seconds. Strain into a Collins glass filled with ice and top with club soda. Stir gently with a bar spoon and garnish with a slice of strawberry and basil leaves.

ELAIN'S GARDEN MOCKTAIL

INGREDIENTS

- 1 teaspoon rose syrup (such as Monin Rose Syrup)
- 1 teaspoon elderflower syrup (such as Monin Elderflower Syrup)
- 1 teaspoon lavender syrup (such as Monin Lavender Syrup)
- 5 fluid ounces lemonade
- 2 fluid ounces club soda
- Strawberry slice and basil leaves, for garnish

METHOD

Fill a cocktail shaker halfway with ice, then add rose syrup, elderflower syrup, lavender syrup, and lemonade. Shake for 30 to 60 seconds. Strain into a Collins glass filled with ice and top with club soda. Stir gently with a bar spoon and garnish with a slice of strawberry and basil leaves.

POOL
OF
STARLIGHT

A sip of this will have you feeling like you're living your happily ever after. (Even better if it's proffered by a brooding and haughty lord.) Refreshing and cool, this cocktail will make you feel things you've never felt before.

INGREDIENTS

    2 fluid ounces Pimm's No. 1
    5 fluid ounces lemon-lime soda
    ½ fluid ounce lemon juice, freshly squeezed
    Cucumber slice, strawberry slice, and mint leaves, for garnish

METHOD

In a highball glass filled with ice, add the Pimm's No. 1. Next, add the lemon-lime soda and lemon juice. Stir gently with a bar spoon until combined. Finish by adding more ice as needed, and garnish with slices of cucumber and strawberry, and mint leaves.

FAERIE WINE
IN THE
SPRING COURT

A bubbly cocktail that will make you dance like it's your first summer solstice. Be careful not to overindulge, lest you dance like Feyre in the Spring Court in front of your guests!

TIP: *The glitter is optional for overall flavor, but it's not optional for overall fun. If you want to cut down on the alcohol, you can substitute the elderflower liqueur for 1 teaspoon of elderflower syrup.*

INGREDIENTS

1 fluid ounce elderflower liqueur (such as St-Germain)
Edible glitter (optional)
5 fluid ounces prosecco
Mint sprig, for garnish

METHOD

Add elderflower liqueur and glitter to a champagne flute or coupe glass and gently stir with a bar spoon to combine. Top with prosecco. Lightly stir to combine all ingredients. Garnish with a mint sprig.

THE RHYSAND

Rhysand enters as a graceful and dangerous stranger. As his complex, labyrinthian soul begins to unveil, the most powerful High Lord in Prythian is more tender, playful, and gracious than was once realized. This cocktail pays homage to Rhys's defining traits, like strength, sophistication, and poise, and showcases his signature scents of jasmine, citrus, and sea salt.

INGREDIENTS

- 1½ fluid ounces strongly brewed jasmine green tea, cooled to room temperature
- 1 fluid ounce orange liqueur (such as Cointreau or Grand Marnier)
- 1 fluid ounce orange juice, freshly squeezed
- 1 fluid ounce tequila
- Orange slice, for garnish
- Sea salt for the rim

METHOD

Brew tea using one tea bag in 1½ fluid ounces of hot water, then let cool. Once cooled, in a shaker three-quarters full of ice, add the tea, orange liqueur, orange juice, and tequila. Shake for 15 to 30 seconds. Rub one-fourth of the rim of a martini glass with your orange slice and sprinkle with coarse ground sea salt. Strain the contents of the shaker into the glass and garnish with an orange slice.

AMARANTHA

Unlike the name might suggest, sipping this drink won't be torture. This whiskey cocktail is a nod to both her deep red hair and her even more deeply seated need for the blood of those who would deny her. Drink with caution, as none but Feyre can handle too many rounds with this evil queen.

INGREDIENTS

- 2 fluid ounces whiskey
- 1 fluid ounce amaretto
- 1 fluid ounce orange liqueur (such as Cointreau or Grand Marnier)
- ¼ fluid ounce bourbon cherry juice (from bourbon cherries such as Collins Bourbon Cherries or Woodford Reserve Bourbon Cherries)
- Bourbon cocktail cherry, for garnish

METHOD

In a shaker filled halfway with ice, add the whiskey, amaretto, orange liqueur, and bourbon cherry juice. Shake the contents for 10 to 15 seconds, then strain into a rocks glass filled with ice. Garnish with a bourbon cherry.

UNDER THE MOUNTAIN MOCKTAIL

Tart, striking, and unforgettable, similar to Amarantha's rule Under the Mountain, this is not a mocktail for the weak of heart. This layered cocktail acts as a precise delineation of the fifty years of bloodshed beneath the mountain.

TIP: *Pouring an ingredient "over the back of a spoon" is a common technique for layering ingredients in a layered cocktail. It disperses the liquid over a larger surface area, helping to keep the liquids separate.*

INGREDIENTS

> **5 fluid ounces ginger beer**
> **2 fluid ounces tart cherry juice**
> **Cherry, for garnish**

METHOD

Fill a pint glass with ice and top with ginger beer. Next, place a spoon upside-down across the top of the pint glass, hovering over the ginger beer. Angle the spoon toward the side of the pint glass, and slowly and gently pour tart cherry juice over the back of the spoon to create a layered effect. Top with a cherry.

NESTA'S DIRTY MARTINI

Like stone-faced Nesta, this is a cocktail that seems more intimidating than it is. Deep down this drink is a loyal staple, made of quality ingredients, that will always be there for you when the going gets tough.

TIP: *You can use your favorite olive of choice, but Spanish queen olives create a martini fit for a queen.*

INGREDIENTS

    2 fluid ounces vodka, ideally chilled
    1 fluid ounce olive brine
    ½ fluid ounce dry vermouth
    Olive, for garnish

METHOD

Fill a martini glass with ice and water and set aside. Grab a shaker and fill it three-quarters full with ice. Add vodka and olive brine to the shaker and shake for 10 to 20 seconds. Remove the ice water from the martini glass and add your vermouth. Swirl the vermouth around the glass before dumping the vermouth out. Strain the contents of the shaker into the martini glass and garnish with an olive.

THE WYRM

This is a delicious nod to a dangerous night Feyre spent fighting for her life, and for the future of Prythian, Under the Mountain. The Middengard Wyrm is far more aggressive (and much less appetizing) than this affable, chocolate-topped concoction.

TIP: *If you want to really take this theme to the max, garnish with the dark chocolate topping and add a gummy worm pierced with white toothpicks across the top.*

INGREDIENTS

1 fluid ounce vodka

1 fluid ounce coffee liqueur (such as Kahlúa)

1½ fluid ounces Irish cream (such as Baileys Irish Cream or homemade recipe found on page 15)

1½ fluid ounces heavy cream

1½ teaspoon grated dark chocolate, for garnish (optional)

Gummy worm, for garnish (optional)

METHOD

In a shaker filled halfway with ice, add vodka, coffee liqueur, Irish cream, and heavy cream. Shake for 10 to 15 seconds. Strain into a martini glass. Optional to top with grated chocolate and gummy worm.

WINTER SOLSTICE
IN THE
SPRING COURT

The Spring Court's attempt to celebrate the Winter Solstice may have been a failure, but this bubbly libation is a victory every time. Like Ianthe's grasp on Tamlin, this cocktail has cheerful notes on the surface, with a nearly undetectable dash of bitterness hidden underneath. The rosemary garnish will intoxicate with the scent of evergreen, unifying the flavors with the sweet notes of spring.

INGREDIENTS
   2 fluid ounces limoncello
   4 fluid ounces prosecco
   1 fluid ounce club soda
   Dash of orange bitters
   Rosemary sprig, for garnish

METHOD
In a champagne flute or coupe glass, add limoncello, prosecco, club soda, and bitters. Garnish with a rosemary sprig.

THE NIGHT COURT

Just like the delicate equilibrium of the expansive Night Court, there are two sides to this cocktail. To possess the balance of the Court of Dreams and the Court of Nightmares, you must balance both your sweet and bitter sides.

INGREDIENTS

   2 fluid ounces jasmine green tea–infused gin (page 11)
   ½ fluid ounce lemon juice, freshly squeezed
   1 fluid ounce limoncello
   4 dashes of orange bitters
   Splash of simple syrup
   Lemon slice, for garnish

METHOD

Add the infused gin, lemon juice, limoncello, orange bitters, and simple syrup to a shaker filled with ice and shake for 30 seconds. Strain into a coupe glass and garnish with a slice of lemon.

RHYSAND'S CALMING TEA

Nonalcoholic

Sometimes you feel the ache for a nice cup of tea, and there is nothing better than one made by Rhysand himself. Just one sip of this warm, sweetened tea will settle your mind and help you feel more at ease.

TIP: *For a beverage truly fit for Fae, froth the milk to add extra creaminess to this concoction.*

INGREDIENTS

8 fluid ounces strongly brewed Earl Grey tea (8 fluid ounces hot water to 2 tea bags)

2 fluid ounces milk of choice

½ teaspoon lavender syrup (such as Monin Lavender Syrup)

1 teaspoon vanilla syrup (such as Monin Vanilla Syrup)

METHOD

Start by brewing the tea and set aside. Warm the milk in the microwave for 30 seconds. In a mug, add the warmed milk, lavender syrup, and vanilla syrup. Froth or stir to combine. Pour tea over the milk mixture and enjoy.

SWEET SCENT OF FREEDOM

SERVES 2 TO 3

Nonalcoholic

When Feyre is rescued from the Spring Court, she has the feeling of summer and experiences the bright sugary scent of strawberry before being swept to refuge in the Night Court. This nonalcoholic drink will give you that same sweet, refreshing taste of freedom.

INGREDIENTS

½ pound fresh strawberries, hulled and halved
½ large lime, juiced
1 cup water
¼ can (3½ fluid ounces) sweetened condensed milk

METHOD

Add strawberries, lime juice, water, and sweetened condensed milk to a blender and blend until smooth. Pour over ice and enjoy.

NOTE: *To make this drink a little less pure, here's a boozy take. Take 6 fluid ounces of your Sweet Scent of Freedom and add 2 fluid ounces of coconut rum. Shake in a shaker filled halfway with ice and pour over ice into a Collins glass. Garnish with a slice of strawberry and a slice of lime.*

MOR'S CITRUS AND CINNAMON

A perfect balance of sweet and serious, partaking in more than a few of these cocktails will have you sharing all of your truths. Morrigan herself has certainly danced the night away at Rita's with this inebriant in hand. This simple drink has "Mor" layers of complexity than you might realize, much like the Night Court's third-in-command.

INGREDIENTS

2 fluid ounces bourbon
1 fluid ounce orange juice, freshly squeezed
1½ tablespoons pure maple syrup
Pinch of ground cinnamon
Orange twist and cinnamon stick, for garnish

METHOD

Fill a cocktail shaker with ice, then add bourbon, orange juice, maple syrup, and cinnamon. Shake well for 10 to 15 seconds. Strain into a rocks glass filled with ice. Garnish with an orange twist and cinnamon stick.

SUMMER COURT WINE

This sparkling sangria is very easy to love and will quickly become your new favorite drink of the summer . . . court.

INGREDIENTS

1 orange, sliced

2 limes, sliced

1 lemon, sliced

4 strawberries, hulled and halved

4 fluid ounces elderflower liqueur (such as St-Germain)

2 fluid ounces bourbon

2 fluid ounces orange liqueur (such as Cointreau or Grand Marnier)

1 (25 fluid ounces) bottle prosecco

1 (12 fluid ounces) can lemon-lime soda

4 fluid ounces club soda

Sliced strawberries, for garnish

METHOD

Place all of the sliced fruit into a large glass container or pitcher. Add elderflower liqueur, bourbon, and orange liqueur. Slowly add the bottle of prosecco, lemon-lime soda, and club soda, then stir gently. Serve over ice in a wine glass with sliced strawberries for garnish.

THE CASSIAN

A dark and brooding drink named for a dark and brooding male, perfected for the most prized Illyrian warrior. Created with his mate in mind, the coffee liqueur helps to keep up with all the demands and requirements of being mated to a legionnaire of Cassian's caliber.

TIP: *To bring this drink even closer to perfection, flourish with a red Siphon (or a bourbon cherry) on top.*

INGREDIENTS

    2 fluid ounces vodka
    1 fluid ounce coffee liqueur (such as Kahlúa)
    Bourbon cherries (such as Collins Bourbon Cherries or
        Woodford Reserve Bourbon Cherries), for garnish

METHOD

In a rocks glass filled with ice, add vodka and coffee liqueur. Stir with a bar spoon for 30 seconds to combine. Garnish with bourbon cherries.

THE AZRIEL

This recipe is a take on a Dark and Stormy, which is the perfect way to describe everyone's beloved Illyrian shadowsinger spymaster. The cocktail's beautiful golden hue will leave you feeling like you're looking right into Azriel's breathtaking hazel eyes.

INGREDIENTS

    2 fluid ounces dark rum
    ½ fluid ounce lime juice, freshly squeezed
    2 dashes of orange bitters
    5 fluid ounces ginger beer
    Lime wheel, for garnish

METHOD

In a Collins glass filled with ice, add rum, lime juice, and bitters. Top with ginger beer and stir gently with a bar spoon to combine. Garnish with a lime wheel.

THE BLOODY AMREN

Though Amren would prefer this warm . . . and from a goat, this is the perfect bloody drink for a mortal. You'll find a layered balance of richness and spices designed to impress even the finest Fae palate.

TIP: *You can substitute vodka for tequila, but this version provides a much-needed twist. Much like Amren's storyline, it will not disappoint.*

INGREDIENTS

3 fluid ounces tequila

¾ cup tomato juice

½ fluid ounce lemon juice, freshly squeezed

½ fluid ounce olive juice

½ fluid ounce pickled pepperoncini juice

3 dashes of Worcestershire sauce

5 dashes of hot sauce

¼ teaspoon celery seed

¼ teaspoon seasoned salt and freshly ground black pepper

Lemon wedge, pepperoncini, and olive, for garnish

METHOD

Fill a shaker halfway with ice. Add tequila, tomato juice, lemon juice, olive juice, pepperoncini juice, Worcestershire sauce, hot sauce, celery seed, salt, and black pepper, then shake for 30 seconds. Strain into a Collins glass filled with ice and add more hot sauce and seasoned salt to taste. Garnish with a lemon wedge, pepperoncini, and olive.

MINT TEA JULEP

If you're pining for access to the inner circle of the Night Court, it is important to find a favored tea drink. On more than one occasion, Feyre is found sipping mint tea to get through an unpredictable Prythian existence with her mate. In this cocktail, adding some bourbon can bring ease to any uncomfortable situation.

INGREDIENTS

> 3 fluid ounces strongly brewed mint tea (such as Numi
>   Moroccan Mint tea), cooled to room temperature
> 2½ fluid ounces bourbon
> 1 fluid ounce simple syrup
> Mint sprig, for garnish

METHOD

Brew tea and let cool. Once cooled, add tea to a shaker filled with ice, then add the bourbon and simple syrup. Shake for 30 seconds. Strain into a Collins glass filled with ice and garnish with a mint sprig.

CHILLED MINT TEA MOCKTAIL

Nonalcoholic

Delicious and refreshing, this mocktail will have you asking for another round.

TIP: *If you like things a little sweeter, you can adjust the amount of amaretto syrup to your liking.*

INGREDIENTS

> 4 fluid ounces mint tea (such as Numi Moroccan Mint tea),
> cooled to room temperature
> 1 teaspoon amaretto syrup (such as Monin Amaretto Syrup)
> 1 fluid ounce club soda
> Mint sprig, for garnish

METHOD

Brew tea and let cool. In a highball glass filled with ice, add the mint tea and amaretto syrup. Stir with a bar spoon to combine. Top with club soda and garnish with a mint spring.

SUMMER COURT MOCKTAIL

There is nothing like a cold, bubbly drink when you're sitting out in the sun of the Summer Court, and this drink is sure to hit the spot. This mocktail will help you keep your wits about you—key in any Summer Court dalliance.

TIP: *For a twist, try ginger ale in place of the lemon–lime soda.*

INGREDIENTS

> 6 fluid ounces lemon-lime soda
> 1 fluid ounce hibiscus syrup (such as Monin Hibiscus Syrup)
> ½ fluid ounce lime juice, freshly squeezed
> Mint leaves and lime slice, for garnish

METHOD

In a Collins glass filled with ice, add the lemon-lime soda, hibiscus syrup, and lime juice. Stir gently with a bar spoon to combine. Garnish with mint leaves and a lime slice.

THE INVISIBLE
SPECK OF LINT

Not sure what to do with your hands? Feeling like you need to distract and take the intensity out of a charged encounter? Feeling overly confident in a heated argument? If so, this is the perfect drink for you.

TIP: *This recipe also works well with your favorite flavored vodka in place of the plain vodka, if you want to give it your own signature flavor.*

INGREDIENTS
    2 fluid ounces vodka
    2 fluid ounces club soda
    2 fluid ounces lemon-lime soda
    Lemon slice, for garnish

METHOD
In a highball glass filled with ice, add vodka, club soda, and lemon-lime soda. Stir gently with a bar spoon to combine. Garnish with a slice of lemon or any preferred fruit.

STARFALL CELEBRATION COCKTAIL

Mirroring the beauty and magic of the Starfall celebration, best known for its epic festival in Velaris, this cocktail is sweet, bubbly, and twinkling with stars. One sip will have you smiling with genuine merriness.

TIP: *You can add any edible glitter you may have, but a mix of dark and light colors gives a convincing illusion of a sky filled with falling stars.*

INGREDIENTS

- 2 fluid ounces blackberry-infused whiskey (such as Crown Royal Blackberry or Starlight Distillery Blackberry Whiskey, or homemade recipe on page 13)
- 1 fluid ounce orange liqueur (such as Cointreau or Grand Marnier)
- 2 fluid ounces ginger ale
- Edible glitter (black and light blue)

METHOD

In a rocks glass filled with ice, add the blackberry whiskey and orange liqueur. Stir with a bar spoon for 15 to 30 seconds to combine. Add ginger ale and glitter. Stir gently until combined. Top with additional ice to fill the glass, if desired.

THE BLOOD RUBY

A blood ruby should be sent to a mortal enemy to mark them for death, emanating from an act of betrayal. Make sure those who receive the cocktail version know you're not out for blood, just for a good time.

TIP: *If you substitute fresh pomegranate seeds for frozen, serve this cocktail over ice.*

INGREDIENTS

 1½ fluid ounces vodka

 1 fluid ounce orange juice, freshly squeezed

 1 fluid ounce pomegranate juice

 1 fluid ounce elderflower liqueur (such as St-Germain)

 2 dashes of orange bitters

 ¼ cup pomegranate seeds, frozen

 2 fluid ounces club soda, chilled

METHOD

Fill a cocktail shaker with ice. Add vodka, orange juice, pomegranate juice, elderflower liqueur, and orange bitters. Shake for 30 to 45 seconds. Add frozen pomegranate seeds to a rocks glass and strain contents of the shaker over the seeds. Top with club soda. Stir gently with a bar spoon to combine.

THE COURT OF DREAMS COCKTAIL

Light, bright, clean, and delightful, this cocktail will transport you straight to the breathtaking streets of Velaris.

INGREDIENTS

    1 fluid ounce jasmine green tea–infused gin (page 11)
    4 fluid ounces prosecco
    ½ fluid ounce limoncello
    1 fluid ounce club soda
    Lemon slice, for garnish

METHOD

In a champagne flute or coupe glass, add the infused gin, prosecco, limoncello, and club soda. Garnish the glass with a slice of lemon.

ROSE TEA LEMONADE COCKTAIL

If you take only one thing away from the enchanting ACOTAR series, let it be that a good cup of tea can cure just about anything. That fact remains true with this boozy Rose Tea Lemonade, enjoyed over ice.

INGREDIENTS

2 fluid ounces rose tea–infused vodka (page 11)

2½ fluid ounces lemonade

½ fluid ounce elderflower liqueur (such as St-Germain)

3 large fresh basil leaves, plus more for garnish

1½ fluid ounces club soda

Lemon slice, for garnish

METHOD

Fill a cocktail shaker halfway with ice. Add the infused vodka, lemonade, elderflower liqueur, and 3 basil leaves. Shake well for 30 to 60 seconds. Strain into a Collins glass filled with ice and top with club soda. Stir lightly with a bar spoon. Add basil leaves and a lemon slice for garnish.

ROSE TEA LEMONADE MOCKTAIL

Nonalcoholic

INGREDIENTS

- 4 fluid ounces rose tea, cooled to room temperature
- ½ fluid ounce elderflower syrup (such as Monin Elderflower Syrup)
- 3 fluid ounces lemonade
- 1 fluid ounce club soda
- Lemon slice and basil leaves, for garnish

METHOD

Brew rose tea and allow to cool. In a Collins glass filled with ice, add rose tea, elderflower syrup, and lemonade. Stir with a bar spoon to combine, then top with club soda. Garnish with lemon slice and basil leaves.

THE COURT
OF
NIGHTMARES

If you find yourself spending nightfall in the Hewn City under the mountains of the Night Court, it's best to keep your shields up and mind alert. For a mortal, the best solution is to remain heavily caffeinated. This martini will keep you awake while giving you enough liquid courage to make it through till morning.

TIP: *The espresso should be made in advance and cooled to room temp.*

INGREDIENTS
   1 fluid ounce espresso, cooled to room temperature
   2 fluid ounces vodka
   1 fluid ounce coffee liqueur (such as Kahlúa)

METHOD
Fill a martini glass with ice and water and set aside. In a shaker filled with ice, add cooled espresso, vodka, and coffee liqueur. Shake for 30 seconds. Remove the ice water from the martini glass and strain the contents of the shaker into the glass.

WINTER COURT COCKTAIL

The icy flavor of this creamy cocktail will transport you straight to the barren lands of the Winter Court.

TIP: *If you're more frigid-minded, feel free to add an additional ½ fluid ounce of peppermint schnapps and cut back on the coffee liqueur.*

INGREDIENTS
- 1½ fluid ounce peppermint schnapps
- 1 fluid ounce coffee liqueur (such as Kahlúa)
- 1 fluid ounce Irish cream (such as Baileys Irish Cream, or homemade recipe on page 15)
- 1½ fluid ounce heavy cream
- Mint sprig, for garnish

METHOD

In a shaker filled three-quarters with ice, add peppermint schnapps, coffee liqueur, Irish cream, and heavy cream. Shake for 30 to 60 seconds. Strain into a rocks glass filled with ice. Garnish with a sprig of mint.

WINTER COURT MOCKTAIL

INGREDIENTS

> 1½ fluid ounces peppermint syrup (such as Monin Peppermint Syrup)
>
> 1 fluid ounce coffee, cooled to room temperature, or cold brew
>
> 1½ fluid ounces heavy cream
>
> 1 teaspoon vanilla syrup (such as Monin Vanilla Syrup)
>
> Mint sprig, for garnish

METHOD

In a shaker filled three-quarters with ice, add peppermint syrup, coffee, heavy cream, and vanilla syrup. Shake for 30 to 60 seconds. Strain into a rocks glass filled with ice. Garnish with a sprig of mint.

ILLYRIAN BLACK AND TAN ALE

SERVES TWO

Nothing can cure what "ales" you quite like a pint of Illyrian ale. It can relax even the most hardened warrior at the end of a long day of training in the war camp. After a few pints, you might even find yourself sprouting wings and soaring through the mountains.

TIP: *The layer of foam mentioned in the instructions is key to getting the layering effect to hold.*

INGREDIENTS
> **1 (14.9–fluid ounces) can Irish pilsner (such as Harp)**
> **1 (14.9–fluid ounces) can Guinness**

METHOD

Into a pint glass, pour half of the can of Irish pilsner. Try not to be too gentle with it, giving you a layer of foam (about a ½ inch). Next, place a spoon upside-down across the top of the pint glass, hovering above the foam. Angle the spoon toward the side of the pint glass, and slowly and gently pour half the can of Guinness over the backside of the spoon to create the layering of the 2 beers.

HELION'S COCKTAIL

The High Lord of the Day Court is described as the sun itself, and this cocktail is the perfect portrait of his exquisite glare. Helion is eternally open to taking in joy, and a little tequila always enhances a mortal's joyfulness.

INGREDIENTS

2 fluid ounces silver tequila
½ cup orange juice, freshly squeezed
¼ cup pineapple juice
1 fluid ounce grenadine
Orange slice, for garnish

METHOD

Add tequila, orange juice, and pineapple juice to a shaker filled with ice. Shake for 15 to 30 seconds. Strain the mixture into a highball glass filled three-quarters with ice. Next, place a spoon upside-down atop the glass and angle it toward the side of the glass. Slowly pour the grenadine over the back of the spoon into the glass to create a layered effect. Garnish with an orange slice.

SOOTHING BOURBON COCKTAIL

Sometimes you need a stiff bourbon drink to calm your nerves. For example, if you find yourself reflecting after you just raced toward a bottomless pit in your library while being chased by trained assassins trying to kill you and kidnap your sister, causing you to make a high-stakes bargain with the library's bottomless pit monster to save both of your lives . . . this is definitely a good reason for a bourbon drink.

TIP: *This drink can also be enjoyed when you need a nightcap at the end of a long day at your corporate job—no threat of murder required.*

INGREDIENTS

    4 bourbon cocktail cherries (such as Collins Bourbon Cherries or Woodford Reserve Bourbon Cherries), plus 1 for garnish
    ½ lemon, split into 4 wedges
    1 fluid ounce simple syrup
    2½ fluid ounces bourbon
    Lemon twist, for garnish

METHOD

Place 4 cherries, quartered lemon, and simple syrup in an empty cocktail shaker and muddle for 30 seconds. Fill the shaker three-quarters full with ice and add bourbon. Shake for 30 seconds. Strain into a rocks glass filled with ice. Garnish with remaining cherry and a lemon twist.

THE DAWN COURT

Warm, inviting, and refreshing, this concoction is the perfect glowing day drink. You can sip this refreshing pairing of lemonade and cherry from dawn to dusk.

TIP: *You can substitute the bourbon cherry juice for tart cherry juice if you prefer.*

INGREDIENTS

    4 fluid ounces lemonade
    2 fluid ounces vodka
    ½ fluid ounce bourbon cherry juice (such as from Collins Bourbon Cherries or Woodford Reserve Bourbon Cherries)
    1 fluid ounce club soda
    Bourbon cherry, for garnish

METHOD

In a Collins or highball glass filled with ice, add lemonade, vodka, and cherry juice. Stir with a bar spoon to combine and top with club soda. Garnish with a bourbon cherry.

AUTUMN COURT COCKTAIL

The Autumn Court menaces those who seek peace in Prythian, but it also yields bountiful forests and farmland filled with eternal autumnal fruit. A showcase to the beauty and flavors of autumn, this cocktail transports you to the lush golden forests of the fall.

INGREDIENTS

> 2 fluid ounces chai tea–infused bourbon (recipe on page 13)
> 2 fluid ounces apple juice (such as Martinelli's or Simply)
> Apple slice and cinnamon stick, for garnish

METHOD

In a rocks glass filled halfway with ice, add the infused bourbon and apple juice. Stir with a bar spoon to combine and chill. Garnish with an apple slice and cinnamon stick.

AUTUMN COURT MOCKTAIL

Nonalcoholic

A slightly more bubbly and fully nonalcoholic version of the Autumn Court Cocktail, this mocktail gives you all the same flavors and aromas of fall and none of the hangover.

INGREDIENTS

2 fluid ounces chai tea, cooled to room temperature

3 fluid ounces nonalcoholic sparkling apple cider (such as Martinelli's)

Apple slice and cinnamon stick, for garnish

METHOD

Brew the chai tea and let cool. In a highball glass filled with ice, add sparkling apple cider and chai tea. Stir gently with a bar spoon to combine. Garnish with an apple slice and cinnamon stick.

VALKYRIE VODKA SODA

Breathe in through your nose, out through your mouth. Calm your body, mind, and spirit. Once you've found that inner peace, you're on your way to commanding the power of the Valkyries.

NOTE: *A few sips of this mixture will fortify your strength and solidify your warrior spirit. Get ready for battle.*

INGREDIENTS

    2 fluid ounces vodka
    1 fluid ounce grapefruit juice, freshly squeezed
    ¼ fluid ounce vanilla syrup (such as Monin Vanilla Syrup)
    2 fluid ounces club soda
    Grapefruit twist, for garnish

METHOD

In a shaker halfway filled with ice, add vodka, grapefruit juice, and vanilla syrup. Shake for 15 to 30 seconds and strain into a rocks glass filled with ice. Top with club soda. Garnish with a grapefruit twist.

WINTER SOLSTICE HOT COCOA

If you're fortunate enough to celebrate the Winter Solstice with your found family in Velaris, you'll be sure to partake in a few steaming cups of rich and creamy hot cocoa.

TIP: *Add your favorite cocoa accompaniment, such as marshmallow, mint syrup, or, for a boozy version, add peppermint schnapps.*

INGREDIENTS

> 1 cup milk of choice
> 1¾ tablespoons sugar
> 2 teaspoons cocoa powder
> Pinch of salt
> ¼ teaspoon vanilla syrup (such as Monin Vanilla Syrup)

METHOD

In a microwave-safe measuring cup or vessel, warm the milk for 1 minute (or until hot). In a separate mug, add sugar, cocoa powder, and salt. Add the hot milk to the mug, stirring to combine. Add vanilla syrup, stir, and enjoy.

PREFERRED BUBBLY
OF THE COURTS

For each glass of bubbly, start by adding your juice or syrup, then top with prosecco.

SPRING COURT BUBBLY

INGREDIENTS

> 1 teaspoon rose syrup (such as Monin Rose Syrup)
> 5 fluid ounces prosecco

SUMMER COURT BUBBLY

INGREDIENTS

> 1 teaspoon hibiscus syrup (such as Monin Hibiscus Syrup)
> 5 fluid ounces prosecco

AUTUMN COURT BUBBLY

INGREDIENTS

> 1 fluid ounce apple juice (such as Martinelli's or Simply)
> 5 fluid ounces prosecco

WINTER COURT BUBBLY

INGREDIENTS

> 1 fluid ounce cranberry juice
> 5 fluid ounces prosecco

SNACKS
AND
SPREADS

VELARIS DESSERT

You'll feel like you've been transported straight to the City of Starlight with this simple, light, citrusy, and boozy dessert.

INGREDIENTS

1 cup vanilla ice cream
¼ cup limoncello
1 bourbon cherry

METHOD

Scoop the ice cream into a martini glass or bowl. Pour over with limoncello, adding more or less to taste, and top with a cherry.

MEET THE ARCHERON FAMILY MEAL

There is nothing quite like meeting your partner's family for the first time. And it's bound to be even more uncomfortable if you're also discussing an impending war likely to engage on mortal soil.

Though these foods may be bland for a faerie's palate, they're perfectly suited to mortal tastebuds.

TIP: *This is a spread well-suited for brunch.*

INGREDIENTS

2 or 3 jars pickled vegetables (such as beets, carrots, cucumber, asparagus, or green beans)

1 (2-ounce) jar capers

1 (12-ounce) container cream cheese

12 ounces pre-sliced smoked salmon

1 large red onion, thinly sliced

6 hard-boiled eggs, halved and sprinkled with salt and pepper

1 bunch fresh dill, stemmed

1 large lemon, sliced and seeded

1 (8-ounce) block gouda cheese, sliced

Loaf of hearty sourdough or rye bread, sliced

Served on 1 or 2 serving boards

Start your spread by adding the pickled vegetables, capers, and cream cheese to small bowls.

On your serving boards, arrange the smoked salmon, red onion, hard-boiled eggs, dill, lemon, cheese, bread, and bowls. Add small spoons, forks, and cheese knives for serving.

SUMMER COURT TOMATO TARTS

12 Tomato Tarts

DOUGH INGREDIENTS

1 package (2 sheets) frozen puff pastry
2 heirloom tomatoes, sliced ¼ inch thick
10 to 12 cherry tomatoes, halved
Salt

FILLING INGREDIENTS

½ cup mayonnaise
¼ cup full-fat sour cream
1 cup mozzarella cheese
1 cup cheddar cheese
12 basil leaves, chiffonade
2 green onions, diced to the white
2 cloves garlic, minced
1 tablespoon flat-leaf parsley, minced
1 teaspoon salt
1 teaspoon pepper
1 egg
1 teaspoon water

METHOD

Thaw frozen puff pastry to package instructions (usually around 40 minutes).

During those 40 minutes, place the sliced heirloom tomatoes in a colander in the sink and sprinkle with salt to pull out some moisture.

To create the filling, combine mayonnaise, sour cream, cheeses, basil, green onions, garlic, parsley, and salt and pepper in a medium mixing bowl and stir well to combine. Set in fridge until puff pastry is thawed.

Preheat oven to 400°F for 5 to 10 minutes before puff pastry is thawed.

Transfer the heirloom tomatoes from the colander to a tea towel or paper towel to remove additional moisture.

Once thawed, lay out the puff pastry and press lightly with your fingers to make sure there are no creases in the dough. Cut the sheets into 6 even rectangles from each sheet, creating 12 rectangles.

For the egg wash, combine the egg and water, beat in small bowl, and set aside. Line two baking sheets with parchment paper and place the 12 pieces of puff pastry onto the baking sheets. Use a fork to press down the edges of each pastry about ½ inch in. Brush the edges with the egg wash mixture.

Lay one slice of heirloom tomato on each piece of puff pastry, making sure to leave a ½-inch border. Top each evenly with the filling, and sprinkle halved cherry tomatoes on top.

Place in the oven for 35 to 40 minutes until edges are golden brown.

SPRING COURT CRUDITÉS WITH SPRING HERB DRESSING

SERVES 4–8

SPRING HERB DRESSING INGREDIENTS

4 heaping tablespoons chopped fresh herbs (such as chives, green onion, dill, parsley, or basil)

1 cup mayonnaise

1 cup sour cream

1 cup buttermilk

2 teaspoons distilled white vinegar

2 teaspoons lemon juice, freshly squeezed

1 heaping teaspoon garlic powder

1 heaping teaspoon onion powder

1 teaspoon jarred garlic

¼ teaspoon white pepper

1 teaspoon salt

CRUDITÉS INGREDIENTS

carrots, bell pepper, cucumber, broccoli or your preferred crudités vegetable

METHOD

Roll and pile your herbs, and very finely mince all of them together. (You don't want to know where one herb ends and the next begins.) Place into a large mixing bowl.

Next, add mayonnaise, sour cream, buttermilk, vinegar, lemon juice, garlic powder, onion powder, garlic, white pepper, and salt to the same mixing bowl with the herbs. Stir well to combine, then whisk until no lumps or dry herbs remain visible.

Place into an airtight container and refrigerate for at least 1 hour before serving.

Serve with crudités such as carrots, bell pepper, cucumber, and broccoli.

DAWN COURT MEETING SPREAD

Should you ever find yourself hosting the High Lords of Prythian, follow Thesan's lead and create a beautiful spread of pastries, cured meats, and fruits.

TIP: *This spread also works well for mortal gatherings.*

INGREDIENTS

> 12 to 24 ounces cured meats (such as prosciutto, salami, bresaola, mortadella, or pancetta)
>
> 8 to 16 assorted small pastries (such as croissants, eclairs, puff pastry, pain au chocolat, or macarons)
>
> 12 to 24 ounces fruit (such as raspberries, strawberries, blueberries, or grapes), washed
>
> Served on 1 or 2 serving boards

Begin by arranging your cured meats into roses. The only additional tool required is a wine glass. Taking one slice of meat at a time, gently drape the slice over the rim of the wine glass. Let the edges hang halfway over the edge of the rim. Complete a row around the glass to create the first layer of the rose.

Continue to drape additional slices over the original row, overlapping slightly with each new slice. Continue in the circular pattern, making sure that each slice slightly covers the previous one. This will mimic the petals of a rose.

Once you've layered enough meat to your floral satisfaction, carefully invert and remove the wine glass and place the rose on your charcuterie board. You may need to adjust the shape once you've placed it on the board to create the perfect rose.

Next, arrange the cured meats and pastries on 1 to 2 large boards. Place fruit throughout, filling any empty spaces on the boards.

WINTER SOLSTICE CHARCUTERIE BOARD

SERVES 4 TO 8

There is nothing quite like celebrating winter holidays with friends and family. When you find yourself sharing time and a table with loved ones, just like the Winter Solstice enjoyed in the faerie courts, impress all with this seasonal spread.

INGREDIENTS

- **12 to 24 ounces assorted cheeses (such as goat cheese, Gorgonzola, Gouda, or Parmigiano-Reggiano)**
- **2 boxes assorted crackers**
- **12 ounces pitted medjool dates**
- **1 (10-ounce) jar olives (such as Castelvetrano or kalamata)**
- **1 (10-ounce) jar fig jam**

METHOD

Arrange the cheeses and crackers on 1 to 2 large serving platters. Place dates and olives throughout, filling any empty spaces on the serving platters. Add the fig jam in the original jar along with a small spoon for serving.

Pairings to Entertain

Spring Court Crudités with Spring Herb Dressing with Faerie Wine in the Spring Court

Meet the Archeron Family Meal with flights of the Preferred Bubbly of the Courts, The Bloody Amren, and Helion's Cocktail

Winter Solstice Charcuterie Board with the Winter Solstice Hot Cocoa and Winter Solstice in the Spring Court

Dawn Court Meeting Spread with Elain's Garden and Nesta's Dirty Martini

Summer Court Tomato Tarts with Summer Court Wine
and Summer Court Mocktail

Velaris Dessert with Feyre Darling and The Rhysand

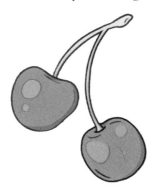

Meet the Archeron Family Meal with Feyre Darling,
Elain's Garden Mocktail, and Nesta's Dirty Martini

Feyre Darling with Tamlin Tequila Cocktail
and The Rhysand

Winter Solstice Charcuterie Board with The Cassian,
The Azriel, and Illyrian Black and Tan Ale

Dawn Court Spread with Autumn Court Cocktail,
Autumn Court Mocktail, Winter Court Cocktail, and
Winter Court Mocktail

NOTES

NOTES

NOTES

NOTES

NOTES

NOTES

NOTES

NOTES

NOTES

NOTES

NOTES

NOTES

Andrews McMeel Publishing
a division of Andrews McMeel Universal
1130 Walnut Street, Kansas City, Missouri 64106

www.andrewsmcmeel.com

25 26 27 28 29 VEP 10 9 8 7 6 5 4 3 2 1

ISBN: 979-8-8816-0197-3

Library of Congress Control Number: 2024948953

Illustrations by Joel Friday

Editor: Charlie Upchurch
Art Director: Holly Swayne
Production Editors: Jasmine Lim, Brianna Westervelt
Production Manager: Julie Skalla

ATTENTION: SCHOOLS AND BUSINESSES
Andrews McMeel books are available at quantity discounts with bulk purchase
for educational, business, or sales promotional use. For information,
please e-mail the Andrews McMeel Publishing Special Sales Department:
sales@andrewsmcmeel.com.